GROUNDCOVER
SERIES

Acknowledgements

The photographer and publisher would like to thank the following for their kind assistance during the development of this book: Holy Trinity Church, Goodramgate (Holy Trinity Church is in the care of The Churches Conservation Trust); Rev. Gant, All Saints' Church, North Street; Richard Masefield at Bar Convent Museum; Peter Brown at Fairfax House; Louise Hampson, Collection Manager, at York Minster.

Text research: David McDonald and Chris Carr for Curran Publishing Services

Neil Jinkerson

Front cover picture: York Minster, from Queen's Walk
Back cover picture: Lendal Tower and Lendal Bridge

Designed and produced by
Jarrold Publishing,
Whitefriars, Norwich NR3 1TR

All photographs
© Neil Jinkerson and Jarrold
Publishing.

© Jarrold Publishing 2002

ISBN 0-7117-1614-5

Printed in Belgium.

1/02

PUBLISHER'S NOTE
Variant and archaic spellings have been retained in quoted material, while the modern spellings of place-names have been used in headings.
   The inclusion of a photograph in this book does not necessarily imply public access to the building illustrated.

YORK

Neil Jinkerson

JARROLD publishing

King's Arms, King's Staith

YORK

GROUNDCOVER
SERIES

Statue of Constantine, York Minster

Contents

Norwich Union Building, Lendal Bridge

Introduction

With its rich architectural legacy and its magnificent Minster, York remains one of England's most cherished cities.

The Romans founded York in AD71 building a legionary fortress which was to be named 'Eboracum'. They were to occupy the site for a further 400 years.

From early times the city began to witness numerous changes to its name: the Anglo-Saxons called it 'Eoforwic', the Vikings 'Jorvik' and the Normans 'York'.

Among the many distinctive features of York are the elevated medieval walls, punctuated by the four original gateways: Bootham Bar, Micklegate Bar, Monk Bar and Walmgate Bar. The Bar Walls (thought to be derived from the word 'barrier'), have all remained for centuries relatively untouched, surviving social and historical events such as the Reformation and the English Civil War. It was during this latter period that the city began to decline in prominence due to the social and political upheaval of the times.

However, during the eighteenth and nineteenth centuries York flourished once more with the building of townhouses, the arrival of the railways and the development of the chocolate industry, led by businesses of Terry and Rowntree.

Throughout the years York was to become increasingly recognised as one of the best-preserved cities in England and, despite its huge popularity, has retained its character and charm.

Stroll around the city and you will come across numerous listed buildings, from the medieval Clifford's Tower to the refined elegance of Fairfax House, one of the finest Georgian houses in England.

While York can boast beautiful buildings, many of which have been there for centuries, it is a vibrant city – a thriving centre for commerce and education. The daily bustle among the shops, restaurants and pubs of Stonegate and the Shambles is a reminder of this.

York offers each visitor the unique opportunity to explore history through the diverse architecture along its delightful streets and medieval passage-ways, amidst a lively cultural scene.

STONEGATE

York's not so great as Old
    York was of yore,
Yet York it is though wasted
    to the core:
It's not that York which
    Ebrank built of old;
Nor yet that York which was
    of Roman mould;
York was the third time
    burnt, and what you see
Are York's small ashes of
    antiquity.

Sir THOMAS WIDDRINGTON
Quoted in E. BAINE,
Baine's Yorkshire, vol.2
1969

STONEGATE

The grand meeting of the nobility and gentry of the north…is now at York in or about the month of August; drawn hither by the hopes of being agreeably entertained, for a week, in horse-racing, balls, assemblies, &c. Horse racing draws in the country people in vast crowds, but the gentry, nay even the clergy and prime nobility are mixed among them.

FRANCIS DRAKE *Eboracum* 1736

SHIP'S FIGUREHEAD
STONEGATE

A ship's figurehead on Kilvington's shop in Stonegate recalls the days when York was a flourishing port. Many of York's timbered houses were built from timbers taken from ships abandoned at the city quays.

YE OLDE STARRE INNE
STONEGATE

The Olde Starre Inne is believed to have been named after King Charles I whose nickname was the Old Star. Dick Turpin and Guy Fawkes are just a few of the famous names to have visited the inn over the years.

DOCTOR'S SIGN
STONEGATE

I have reached this great town safe, and am not wearied with walking, but the better for it. And I have seen many things which I trust to tell you one day, also the muckle kirk of this place; and all around the city are mills whilk have na' muckle wheels nor mill-dams, but gang by the wind and strange to behold …

I wish I kend onything that wad mak ye weel, for they hae mair medicines in this Town of York than wad cure a' Scotland, and surely some of them wad be gude foe your complaints.

SIR WALTER SCOTT
The Heart of Midlothian
1818

RED DEVIL
STONEGATE

Amongst the delightful street of Stonegate with its bustling shops, old inns and Victorian buildings lingers the figure of a small red devil. Its history is uncertain, though it is often said to represent a printer's devil – 'devils' were printers' inky errand boys.

FACE
Coney Street

From the neat and accurate typography of [the] 'two lean volumes'—'price 5s. neatly bound' … it is accepted that [the] first two parts of Tristram Shandy were printed in Coney Street by Ann Ward and David Russell in January, 1760 … If in the words of J.B. Priestley, 'Modern literature begins with Sterne', then the printing of modern literature began in York.

WILLIAM K. SESSIONS
Quoted in A. STACPOOLE,
The Noble City of York
1972

BARLEY HALL
Stonegate

Hidden away down the tiny Coffee Yard, off Stonegate, stands Barley Hall, a medieval town house built in 1316. Having been neglected over time, restoration of the hall has returned it to its former glory complete with medieval-style furniture and hangings.

ST HELEN'S SQUARE

Terry's Restaurant, by the firm's own architectural department, in St Helen's Square, with a giant order and in good ashlar, fits happily between the Yorkshire Insurance building and the Savings bank, and the large range, including Betty's, in neo-Georgian style by T. P. Bennet and interior fittings by Ward and Leckenby, ... are quite gracious and will weather well.

ERIC A. GEE
Quoted in A. STACPOOLE,
The Noble City of York
1972

This building in St Helen's Square was once Terry's Restaurant.

ST HELEN'S SQUARE

The city corporation bought St Helen's churchyard in 1733 and paved it to give the gentry better access to their carriages to the nearby Assembly Rooms. The buildings are mostly Georgian, though the southern side was developed in the 1920s. St Helen's Church dates from the thirteenth and fourteenth centuries, and has a curious font: its base is from the thirteenth century, its capital from the fifteenth, and its bowl from the twelfth.

MANSION HOUSE
ST HELEN'S SQUARE

The residence of the Lord
Mayor is the Mansion House, a
stately edifice, built in the year
1726, and which stands at the
north end of Coney Street, near
Lendal, and occupies the site of
the ancient chapel of the guild
of St. Christopher.

E. BAINE
Baine's Yorkshire, vol.2
1969

MANSION HOUSE
ST HELEN'S SQUARE

… the press-gang had no easy
time of it on the Yorkshire coast.
In other places they inspired fear,
but here rage and hatred. The
Lord Mayor of York was warned
on 20th January, 1777, by an
anonymous letter, that 'if those
men were not sent from the city
on or before the following
Tuesday, his lordship's own
dwelling, and the Mansion-house
also, should be burned to the
ground'.

ELIZABETH GASKELL
Sylvia's Lovers
1863

BETTY'S
St Helen's
Square

Created by the same
designers who shaped
the interiors of the *Queen
Mary* translantic liner,
Betty's is a classic English
tea room offering an
assortment of sweet
temptations within a
cosy environment.

ST SAMPSON'S
CHURCH STREET

St Sampson, Church Street, is [first] mentioned in 1152. In 1444 Thomas Karr left twenty marks to rebuild the north aisle in the same way that the south aisle had just been built. It is probable that the best features in the church, an arch-braced roof over the main span and one old roof truss in the south aisle, were fitted at the time. In 1485 money was left towards building the tower, which itself was injured long afterwards by cannon balls in 1644. There was a fire in 1842/3 serious enough to necessitate a rebuilding of everything in 1848 except the tower.

ERIC A. GEE
Quoted in A. STACPOOLE,
The Noble City of York
1972

THE HOUSE OF
MARGARET CLITHEROW
WHO WAS MARTYRED IN YORK
MARCH 25th 1586
CANONISED OCTOBER 25th 1970
ENTRANCE IN SHAMBLES

HOUSE OF MARGARET CLITHEROE
THE SHAMBLES

The house which is dedicated to Margaret Clitheroe is an exceptional fourteenth century house with a roof truss at the back range which is gargantuan, and even the front gable is of the fifteenth century with its pronounced lean towards an early ditch deep under the ground.

ERIC A. GEE
Quoted in A. STACPOOLE,
The Noble City of York
1972

COTTAGE
Newgate

A great many years ago …
there dwelt, in the ancient city
of York, five maiden sisters …
They were tall stately figures,
with dark flashing eyes and hair
of jet; dignity and grace were in
their every movement; and
the fame of their great beauty
had spread through all the
country round.

CHARLES DICKENS
Nicholas Nickleby
1838

NEWGATE MARKET

In this city there are nominally three market days, namely Tuesday, Thursday, and Saturday, but the principal
market is on Saturday. There is also a market for Swine, held every Wednesday, near Fossbridge.

E. BAINE *Baine's Yorkshire vol.2* 1969

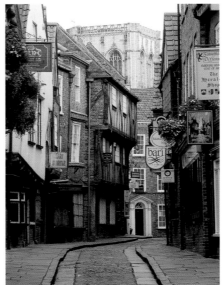

OLD WHITE SWAN
GOODRAMGATE

The streets are lined with numerous pubs. Many of which started life as coaching inns, and still retain their original layout. The Old White Swan has been a public house since 1703 (although it is believed to have been an inn well before this date) and contains nine separate medieval timber-framed structures, inglenook fireplaces and a section of Roman column.

THE SHAMBLES

This is the most famous old street of York, because it is so narrow and so picturesque, particularly where two timber-framed houses almost touch with their overhangs. Hand-shaking ought not to be difficult.

NIKOLAUS PEVSNER
Yorkshire: York and the East Riding
1972

HOLY TRINITY
GOODRAMGATE

Nestled behind Lady Row stands
Holy Trinity. Built in 1316, the
church boasts Jacobean box pews
and a fine fifteenth-century east
window. Secluded within a small
leafy churchyard, it remains a
peaceful haven from the hustle and
bustle of daily life.

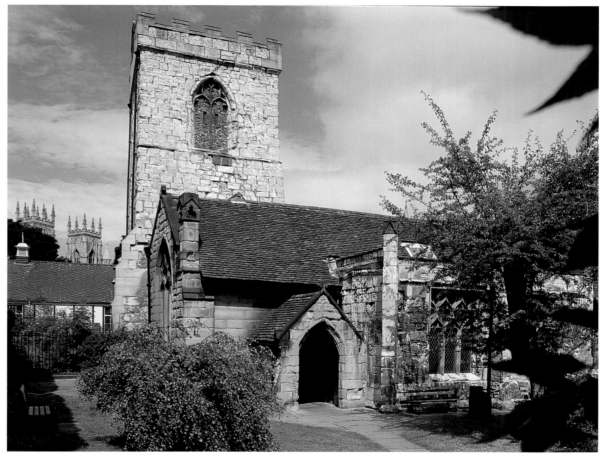

LADY ROW
GOODRAMGATE

(Our) Lady's Row, a short row
of houses on the north-west
side of Goodramgate … was
built in 1316 … The cult of
the Blessed Virgin was always
particularly strong in York
and these houses were built in
order that the rents raised
would pay the salary of a
priest to attend a new chantry
altar in the church, dedicated
to St. Mary from which the
Row takes its name.

R. K. BOOTH
York: The History and Heritage of a City
1990

ROMAN COLUMN

The antiquities indicative of the
long residence of the Romans
here, are less numerous than
might have been supposed, if we
did not take into consideration,
that fire, sword, ignorance and
superstition have all contributed
their assistance to the devouring
hand of time, to erase the
monuments which the imperial
power had served to erect.

E. BAINE
Baine's Yorkshire, vol.2
1969

GUY FAWKES' BIRTHPLACE
STONEGATE

Remember, remember the
    fifth of November
Gunpowder treason and plot,
We see no reason
Why gunpowder treason
Should ever be forgot.

It is believed that Guy Fawkes was born in this building, which is now a hotel.

ST PETER'S SCHOOL

Guy [Fawkes] was born on 16th April, 1570, in York, and attended St. Peter's School … There can be little doubt that his attendance at St. Peter's School brought him into the Gunpowder plot; for three other conspirators were 'Peterites', and they no doubt knew that Guy's military speciality was mining, that is blowing up fortifications.

DAVID CUMMIN
Quoted in A. STACPOOLE,
The Noble City of York
1972

YORK ARMS
HIGH PETERGATE

Yorke, Yorke, for my
   monie,
Of all the cities that I
   ever see,
For merry pastime and
   companie.

OLD BALLAD c.1580
Quoted in E. SLINGSBY,
In Praise of Yorkshire
1951

TOBACCONIST SIGN
LOW PETERGATE

At the French manufacture of
Rapee Snuff, in Lord Irwin's
house at the West end of the
Minster Yard, York, gents and
ladies may be supplied by
Mr. de Boissy with the best
Rapee snuff … as well as with
Scotch Havannah … and
likewise fine smoking tobacco.

E. BAINE
Baine's Yorkshire, vol.2
1969

MINSTER WALLS

This city, first, by Roman
hand was formd,
With lofty towers, and high
built walls adorn'd:
It gave their leaders a secure
repose;
Honour to th' empire,
terror to their foes.

ALCUIN
Quoted in E. BAINE
Baine's Yorkshire, vol.2
1969

Alcuin was an eighth century
Northumbrian scholar and
an adviser to Emperor
Charlemagne.

MINERVA
PETERGATE

[An] impressive shop front at the corner of Minster Gates has the figure of Minerva, goddess of booksellers, above it
… Designed by Francis Wolstenholme, the old sign on the corner of this building is happily visible to this day …

WILLIAM K. SESSIONS   Quoted in A. STACPOOLE, *The Noble City of York*   1972

YORK MINSTER

In 1927, when the minster celebrated its thirteen-hundredth birthday, Archbishop Lang wrote these words:

'Those who were present at the most moving midnight service which ushered in the 1300th year will never forget the sight of the thousands assembled in and around the minster. It seemed as if the deep silent love and pride of the people for the old church had found a sudden and full expression.'

REGINALD CANT
Quoted in A. STACPOOLE,
The Noble City of York
1972

STATUE OF CONSTANTINE
YORK MINSTER

The inauguration of …
Constantine … in the city where
he drew his first breath, serves to
shed an additional lustre on
Eboracum, and has procured for
this ancient city the name of
Altera Roma. The British
soldiers in the pay of Rome
saluted their illustrious
countryman emperor at York…

E. BAINE
Baine's Yorkshire, vol.2
1969

CHOIR SCREEN
YORK MINSTER

The choir screen dividing
the nave is carved with
figures of the kings of
England from William I to
Henry VI.

YORK MINSTER

[For the baptism of Edwin, King of Northumbria in the year 625] … a small oratory of wood, was … erected for the occasion, on the site of the present Cathedral … The ceremony over, … the prelate took care to acquaint the King, that since he had become a Christian, he ought to build a house of prayer, more suitable to the divinity he now adored; and by the bishop's direction, he began to build a magnificent fabric of stone, in the midst of which was inclosed the oratory already erected.

E. BAINE
Baine's Yorkshire, vol.2
1969

YORK MINSTER

Before the Reformation, knights and gentry were entombed under recumbent effigies, their postures formalised: legs crossed for those who had been on Crusade, feet resting on lions for those who had died in battle. Here is a very different image from 1632: Sir William Ingram and his wife, kneeling side by side in Protestant prayer. Sir William had been Secretary to the council of the North that governed the border in King James I's name. His grandson would later marry the daughter of Sir Thomas Fairfax, leader of Parliament's armies against King James' son.

YORK MINSTER

… not only a single
monument to the city and
these northern parts, but to
the whole kingdom.

FRANCIS DRAKE
Eboracum
1736

YORK MINSTER

The accusing spirit, which
flew up to heaven's
chancery with the oath,
blushed as he gave it in;
and the recording angel
as he wrote it down
dropped a tear upon
the word and blotted it
out forever.

LAURENCE STERNE
Tristram Shandy, vol.VII
1759

THE QUEEN'S PATH

The route from the West door of
the York Minster to the Treasurer's
House is named The Queen's Path
in commemoration of the walk
taken by Queen Elizabeth II on
Maundy Thursday in 1972.

GRAY'S COURT

Behind the Treasurer's
House, is Gray's Court. The
house is built on to the
Treasurer's House and
forms a courtyard with it,
open to a beautiful garden
and the city wall beyond.

NIKOLAUS PEVSNER
Yorkshire: York and the East Riding
1972

ST WILLIAM'S COLLEGE

St. William's College['s] quadrangular building is complicated, with many different timber-framed building traditions embodied in it and is of exceptional value. The idea of a college to house the chantry priests of York, who were numerous and living all over the city in relative poverty, was as early as 1419 when Thomas Garton left five marks towards such a building. Not until 1455 was a licence granted to the Archbishop, the Earl of Northumberland and others to found a college of chantry priests in honour of St. William in a house annexed to the canonry or prebend held by the Prior of Hexham.

ERIC A. GEE
Quoted in A. STACPOOLE,
The Noble City of York
1972

ST WILLIAM'S COLLEGE

The desire of knowledge, like the thirst of riches, increases ever with the acquisition of it.

LAURENCE STERNE
Tristram Shandy, vol. II
1759

TREASURER'S HOUSE

During the 1960s a plumber was having his lunch in one of the cellars of the house when … he 'saw a Roman legion march through one of the walls of the cellar and out by another'. The strangest thing was that he said they appeared to be walking on their knees. A few years later the Roman road was discovered — eighteen inches below the present cellar floor, at about the depth that the soldier's feet would have been if their knees had been at the current floor level.

R. K. BOOTH
York: The History and Heritage of a City
1990

MONK'S BAR

The entrance into the city is by four principal gates or bars, and five posterns, or smaller entrances; the gates are Mickelgate-Bar, to the South West, adorned with lofty turrets, finely embattled, over the Roman arch … hangs a large shield, bearing the arms England and France; and on each side one of less size, decorated with the city arms: this is at the entrance from Tadcaster.

E. BAINE
Baine's Yorkshire, vol.2
1969

DE GREY ROOMS
St Leonard's Place

The De Grey rooms in St. Leonard's was built in 1841–2 as an officers' mess for the Yorkshire Hussars and has tall round-headed windows with pediments, a graceful staircase and a lofty hall on the first floor.

ERIC A. GEE
Quoted in A. STACPOOLE,
The Noble City of York
1972

FIREMARK
Bootham Bar

A part of the wall is yet standing in York, which is undoubtedly of Roman erection, and which probably served as an interior fortification to the city. It is the south wall of the Mint-yard, formerly the hospital of St. Lawrence. This erection consists of a multangular tower which leads to Bootham-bar, and a wall which ran the length of Coney or Coning-street, and Castlegate to the Foss.

E. BAINE *Baine's Yorkshire, vol.2* 1969

RED HOUSE (RIGHT) AND CANDLE SNUFFER (BELOW)
DUNCOMBE PLACE

This house was built for Sir William Robinson, Baronet, ancestor of the Marquis of Ripon and M.P. for York… In 1724 the Corporation of York requested that Sir William Robinson should relinquish the Red House, which he held on a very long lease, to become the York Town House, but he refused. Later inhabitants of the house were Dr. John Burton in 1740/6, and in 1814/15 a famous doctor Baldwin Wake resided here.

ERIC A. GEE
Quoted in
A. STACPOOLE,
The Noble City of York
1972

THEATRE ROYAL
BLAKE STREET

The Theatre Royal is conveniently situated in the spacious opening at the upper part of Blake street. The present building was erected by Mr. Joseph Baker, in 1763, in the early part of the theatrical career of Tate Wilkinson, Esq. who in 1769, became manager, under a patent from the crown.

E. BAINE
Baine's Yorkshire, vol.2
1969

YORK CITY ART GALLERY

The Art Gallery is one of the group of buildings near the abbey gardens, and … owes its existence to the persistent hobby of Dr W. A. Evelyn, who for 40 years sought and acquired every York watercolour, pencil drawing, etching, engraving, or lithograph bearing that he could find. This splendid collection was bought for £3000 by public subscription and combined with a hundred pictures left to the Yorkshire fine art institution 50 years earlier by Mr John Burton.

ARTHUR MEE
The King's England –
Yorkshire East Riding and York City
1947

YORKSHIRE MUSEUM

It is the museum that draws all travellers here. Standing finely, with its windows looking on to the river, the collection has been nobly housed on this site for more than a hundred years …

ARTHUR MEE   *The King's England – Yorkshire East Riding and York City* 1947

KING'S MANOR

For the first three hundred years of its history the King's Manor was the palace of the Abbot of St. Mary's Abbey, one of the principal houses of the Benedictine order in the North. For the next hundred years it was the headquarters of the Council of the North and then acquired its present name…

ERIC A. GEE
Quoted in A. STACPOOLE,
The Noble City of York
1972

KING'S MANOR

Over the last three hundred years, the King's Manor has been used for a variety of purposes including the residence of the Governor of York and the Yorkshire School for the Blind. It is presently occupied by the University of York.

ST OLAVE'S CHURCH
MARYGATE

St Olave's Church was founded by Siward, Earl of Northumbria … in 1055 … in memory of his friend, Olaf Haroldsson, to whom the church is dedicated … He and Siward had come to know each other many years before and when … Siward himself died, his heart, if his instructions were carried out, was cut out of his body and buried under the altar of St Olave's Church.

R. K. BOOTH
York: The History and Heritage of a City
1990

ST MARY'S ABBEY
MARYGATE

… the ruin of St. Mary's Abbey, formerly one of the glories of York, and still, 'great in ruin, noble in display,' remains a monument of departed splendour. This once noble and magnificent monastery, is situated on the North side of the city, and the land gently slopes from without Bootham bar to the Ouse … In the year 1270, this Abbey was totally destroyed by fire, but under the direction of Simon de Warwick, the then Abbot, who laid the first stone of the new erection, it again raised its head, and in two and twenty years the identical fabric, of which we this day see the venerable remains was completed.

E. BAINE
Baine's Yorkshire, vol.2
1969

COTTAGE
Marygate

Marygate is associated with the Benedictine Abbey dedicated to the Virgin Mary, which occupied what are now the Yorkshire Museum Gardens and flourished until 1539. It is recorded as Seintemariegate as early as 1354.

R. K. BOOTH
York: The History and Heritage of a City
1990

HOSPITIUM
Marygate

Directions for reviving the 'apparently dead' published by the Humane Society in York:

'WHAT THOU DOEST—DO QUICKLY'

Quoted in E. BAINE *Baine's Yorkshire, vol.2* 1969

YORKSHIRE MUSEUM GARDENS
MARYGATE

Leaving the walls by Lendal
Bridge, we find ourselves by
the Museum Gardens …
They are the gardens of the
York Philosophical Society,
a body of public-spirited
citizens which must be
regarded as the greatest
benefactor of the city. It has
existed since 1822, and its
gardens, covering about ten
acres, have in them the ruins
of a medieval hospital, and a
medieval abbey, the Roman
tower, and the museum
itself.

ARTHUR MEE
*The King's England – Yorkshire East
Riding and York City*
1947

YORKSHIRE MUSEUM GARDENS
MARYGATE

Invention hence her
   compass steers
Towards York, the most
   renowned of shires,
Makes the three Ridings
   in their stories
Each severally to show
   their glories.

M. DRAYTON
Quoted in E. SLINGSBY
In Praise Of Yorkshire
1951

GUILDHALL

… the Martin Bowes Sword, is borne before the
Lord Mayor when he attends the monthly
Council Meeting in the Guildhall … It is said that
when King James VI of Scotland stayed in York at
the King's Manor in 1603 on his way to London
to become James I of Great Britain, the Martin
Bowes sword was carried off 'in mistake' by an
officer of his court. It was recovered only with
difficulty – minus the jewels.

A. L. LAISHLEY
Quoted in A. STACPOOLE, *The Noble City of York*
1972

LENDAL BRIDGE

The bridge is decorated with the two coats of arms of the city. One represents the crossed keys which were given by Christ to St Peter … The other is the red cross of St George on a white background, with five lions.

R. K. BOOTH *York: The History and Heritage of a City* 1990

ST–MARTIN–LE–GRAND
CONEY STREET

The Church of St. Martin, the Bishop, in Coney-street, is an ancient edifice, noticed in Domesday book … The appearance of the exterior of the church is improved by a tower steeple, and it is rendered remarkable by a clock which projects into the street upon which is the figure of a man holding a quadrant that always points to the sun.

E. BAINE   *Baine's Yorkshire, vol.2* 1969

ST MICHAEL
SPURRIERGATE

St Michael's, Spurriergate, stand[s] … amid the roar of traffic at the city's busiest cross-roads. It lost its chancel and part of the nave last century, but it keeps two lofty and leaning arcades from the close of the 12th century, their pointed arches reaching the flat roof and resting on capitals shaped like a cross and carved with leaf ornament.

ARTHUR MEE
The King's England – Yorkshire East Riding and York City
1947

BECKETT ARMS
CONEY STREET

Far to the North, where bold
    Brigantine Kings
Ruled aweful, ere the martial
    clime was hailed
By the loved name of York.

ANON 1809
Quoted in E. SLINGSBY,
In Praise Of Yorkshire
1951

COTTAGE
NORTH STREET

Our ancient and loyal City of York has always been famous for keeping up an hearty and neighbourly way among our selves, which keeps us all friends.

OLD PLAY 1716
Quoted in E. SLINGSBY, *In Praise of Yorkshire*
1951

ALL SAINTS'
NORTH STREET

Turning into North Street, a little road by the Ouse, we come to All Saints', shaded by trees, with timbered house[s] by the churchyard. It is notable for the noblest array of medieval glass in York after the minster, and for its beautiful 15th-century tower, which is square as it rises within the west side of the church.

ARTHUR MEE
The King's England –
Yorkshire East Riding and York City
1947

RAILWAY OFFICE BUILDING

[Preserved in York museum] is a simple human thing that has survived all the mischances of the centuries, the auburn hair of a Roman lady. She was buried in her coffin filled with liquid lime, her head laid on a pillow, and through all the centuries her beautiful hair has remained unspoiled, with the black jet pins still where she put them. When you take a ticket at the booking office in York station you are standing on the spot where, deep beneath your feet, they laid this Roman lady in a coffin with an ornamental covering of lead.

ARTHUR MEE
The King's England – Yorkshire East Riding and York City
1947

RAILWAY STATION

The earliest station is fortunately largely preserved. It is by G. T. Andrews and dates from 1840–2. The main front faces Tanner Row. It is of grey brick with plenty of stone dressings, mostly three-storeyed, with a symmetrical seventeen bay centre. … The centre and ends have ground–floor windows in arched recesses, and the links have Tuscan colonnades. The centre first-floor windows are also arched. Part of the shed – of the simplest iron construction with spidery trusses – also still exists.

NIKOLAUS PEVSNER
Yorkshire: York and the East Riding
1972

YORK RACECOURSE

Next to Newmarket York Races bear the first rank upon the English turf — and if in England, then in the world… horse racing was a favourite amusement in the surrounding forest of Galtres, and as a golden bell, which was tied on the forehead of the winning horse, was the prize, hence the phrase arose of 'bearing away the bell.'

E. BAINE
Baine's Yorkshire, vol. 2
1969

BAR CONVENT MUSEUM

Established as a convent in 1686 by the Institute of the Blessed Virgin Mary, the Bar Convent Museum has many notable features including a beautiful neo-classical chapel, a library of antique books and an archive room which together convey the history of the convent and the nuns who lived there.

MICKLEGATE

The earliest houses in Micklegate are some which were built by the demolished gate of Holy Trinity Priory, two of which remain, and by their features are of fourteenth century date.

ERIC A. GEE
Quoted in A. STACPOOLE,
The Noble City of York
1972

MICKLEGATE BAR

In September 1460, [the Duke of] York made his claim for the throne, only to be defeated and killed at Wakefield the following December. His head was brought to York, topped mockingly with a paper crown, and placed on a spike, first on Ouse Bridge and then on top of Micklegate Bar (the main gate into the city), 'so that York may overlook the town of York', in Shakespeare's words.

R. K. BOOTH
York: The History and Heritage of a City
1990

KING'S STAITH

Stars, ribbons and garters here
loose their lustre strangely,
when the noble peer is dressed
like his groom. But to make
amends for that, view them
at night and their splendour
returns; and here it is that
York shines indeed, when…
a concourse of four or five
hundred of both sexes, out
of the best families in the
kingdom, are met together.
In short, the politeness of the
gentlemen, the richness of the
dress, and remarkable beauty
of the ladies, and, of late, the
magnificence of the room they
meet in, cannot be equalled …
in any part of Europe.

FRANCIS DRAKE
Eboracum
1736

HOLY TRINITY
MICKLEGATE

The old stocks are within
the gates of Holy Trinity,
Micklegate, which stands on
a very early Christian site,
for in the museum is a
tombstone found here
showing a standard-bearer
of the 9th legion with a
Christian symbol above
his head.

ARTHUR MEE
*The King's England – Yorkshire East
Riding and York City*
1947

KING'S STAITH

The name King's Staith is associated with visits to York by kings Edward I, II and III in the thirteenth and fourteenth centuries … Prior to the seventeenth century the staith was referred to as 'the pudding holes', from the Old English pudd meaning 'ditch'. The ditches, dug perpendicular to the river bank at the southern end of the staith, were places where members of the public could bring meat and clothes to be washed …

R. K. BOOTH
York: The History and Heritage of a City
1990

ALMSHOUSES
Skeldergate

The two almshouses were built by public subscription to commemorate Sir Joseph Terry, the Quaker founder of the chocolate dynasty. Terry and Sir Joseph Rowntree were among a generation of Quakers whose companies were founded on improved working conditions and the provision of model housing, open spaces and education.

SKELDERGATE BRIDGE

In 1607, there was a frost of such severity and continuance, that the Ouse became almost a solid body of ice, and a horse race was run on the river, from the Tower, at the end of Marygate, under the great arch of the bridge, to the crane at the Skeldergate postern. Seven years afterwards, there was so heavy a fall of snow, during a frost of about seven weeks, that when it was dissolved by a thaw, the waters of the Ouse so much inundated North-street and Skeldergate, that the inhabitants were obliged to quit their habitations, and to seek safety in more elevated situations.

E. BAINE
Baine's Yorkshire, vol. 2
1969

CASTLE MUSEUM

The Castle Museum was opened
in 1938 and its success in its first
30 years can only be described as
'beyond expectation'.

The main attraction is
undoubtedly the 'street', known
as Kirkgate after its designer, and
the whole idea and conception of
re-erecting shop-fronts to re-
create a street scene of the past is
due to the imaginative planning
of Dr. Kirk.

The shop fronts, windows,
gutters, lamps and miscellaneous
items of street furniture are all
genuine and were acquired for
preservation when the premises
were being demolished or
modernised …

R. PATTERSON
Quoted in A. STACPOOLE, *The Noble City
of York*
1972

DICK TURPIN'S GRAVE

As he went along the streets in the tumbril he bowed to the ladies in the crowds who had come to see him and doffed his hat. Then having arrived at the York Tyburn on the Tadcaster Road, he mounted the ladder to the scaffold and talked to the hangman for half-an-hour before suddenly throwing himself off and into eternity. His body was buried in St. George's churchyard near Fishergate Postern where today a commemorative stone marks the place.

A. L. LAISHLEY   Quoted in A. STACPOOLE, *The Noble City of York* 1972

BONDING WAREHOUSE
SKELDERGATE

The Ouse was used for many purposes. It was a highway for boats, clothes were washed, horses watered and fish gutted. At the Pudding Holes at the end of King's Staith intestines and offal were cleaned for the preparation of black puddings. Dung and refuse were carted down to waiting vessels to be carried away … Water was collected for domestic purposes, and the public privy on Ouse Bridge discharged its contents into the river. It is perhaps not surprising that Andrew Boorde, the sixteenth-century doctor, should have considered that 'water is not good for Englishmen'.

MARGARET C. BARNET
Quoted in A. STACPOOLE, *The Noble City of York* 1972

CLIFFORD'S TOWER
TOWER STREET

During the Commonwealth … there were cannon and powder in Clifford's Tower, and this was to prove disastrous in 1684 when the magazine exploded (owing possibly to careless use of tobacco by one of the guard).

DR. F. W. BROOKS
Quoted in A. STACPOOLE,
The Noble City of York
1972

CLIFFORD'S TOWER
TOWER STREET

The siege of York [in 1643] was … vigorously prosecuted … with an army of from twenty to thirty thousand men; several batteries were opened against the place, and particularly one on a hill, near Walmgate bar, from whence four pieces of cannon played incessantly on the tower, castle, and city, while the garrison, and armed inhabitants, from their different platforms, kept up a heavy fire on the works of the besiegers.

E. BAINE
Baine's Yorkshire, vol. 2
1969

FAIRFAX HOUSE
CASTLEGATE

Fairfax House, Castlegate, was built by
John Carr for the 9th and last Viscount
Fairfax, of Gilling … It has the best series
of rococo ceilings in York, and the main
staircase, of iron, resembles the bottom
flight at Harewood; the same smith,
Maurice Tobin, worked in both houses.

ERIC A. GEE
Quoted in A. STACPOOLE, *The Noble City of York*
1972

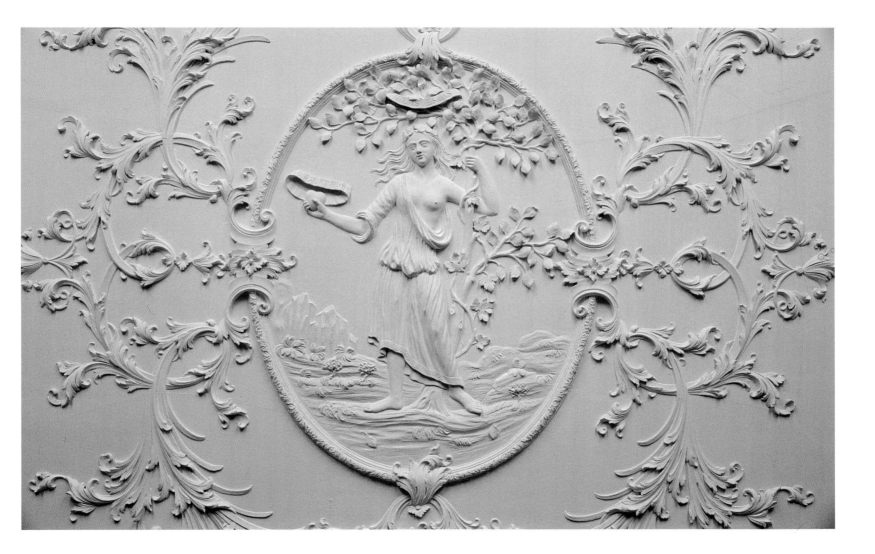

MERCHANT ADVENTURERS' HALL
FOSSGATE

Hither for gain from various
    foreign parts
Come trading people
    seeking opulence
And a secure abode in
    wealthy land

ALCUIN
Quoted in E. BAINE
Baine's Yorkshire, vol. 2
1969

MERCHANT ADVENTURERS' HALL
FOSSGATE

I was born in the Year 1632, in the City of York, of a good Family, tho' not of that Country, my Father being a Foreigner of Bremen, who settled first at Hull: He got a good Estate by Merchandise, and leaving off his Trade, lived afterward at York, from whence he had married my Mother. Relations were named Robinson, a very good Family at Country, and from whom I was called Robinson Keutznaer; but by the usual Corruption of Words in England, we are now called, nay we call our Selves, and write our Name Crusoe, and so my Companions always call'd me.

DANIEL DEFOE
Robinson Crusoe
1720

FOSS BRIDGE

Foss Bridge … was already in existence in some form in the twelfth century, and … seems to have served as the fish market … In the Middle Ages … the lower course of the Foss, below Foss bridge, widened out to form the King's Pool, a large sheet of water which served the mills of the castle and also seems to have supplied fish for the household maintained there.

Dr F. W. BROOKS
Quoted in A. STACPOOLE,
The Noble City of York
1972

CINEMA FRONT
FOSSGATE

[At number 17 Fossgate] the Electric Cinema, neo-Grecian building faced with terracotta tiles, opened in 1907. The screen was at the front of the building and patrons entered by a door on Fossgate and made their way to the back of the hall.

R. K. BOOTH
York: The History and Heritage of a City
1990

ALL SAINTS'
PAVEMENT

The church of All Hallows, commonly called All Saints, … stands partly in High Ousegate, but principally in the Pavement. It is a very ancient structure, and, according to Drake, is built on the ruins of Eboracum. The body of the church and part of the steeple exhibit a very antique appearance, but the edifice is chiefly remarkable for a more modern erection of exquisite Gothic workmanship on the old steeple. This tower is flushed lantern-wise, and tradition says, that anciently a large lamp hung in it, which was lighted in the night time, as a mark for travellers to aim at, in their way to York, over the immense forest of Galtres.

E. BAINE
Baine's Yorkshire, vol. 2
1969

HERBERT HOUSE

Sir Thomas Herbert's House has two overhangs and two gables. The bressumers are decorated, and the gables have pendants. The back wing in Lady Peckitt's Yard is of the 16th century with closely set studs. At the end of the yard is a good brick house of *c.* 1675 with two windows of the Ipswich type.

NIKOLAUS PEVSNER
Yorkshire: York and the East Riding
1972

GOLDEN FLEECE
PAVEMENT

The medieval streets of York are unsurpassed in England for quaintness and interest. When Sydney Smith complained that there was no room for carriages to pass, a driver burst out, 'No room to pass? There's plenty of room, and over an inch to spare.'

ARTHUR MEE *The King's England – Yorkshire East Riding and York City* 1947

WHIP-MA-WHOP-MA GATE
PAVEMENT

Connecting Colliergate with Pavement, this has the double distinction of being the shortest street in York and the street with the longest name. Although popularly interpreted to mean the place where miscreants were whipped, some suggest the original medieval name of 'Whit-Nour-What-Nour-Gate' roughly translates as 'Call that a street – you must be joking!'

YORK or EBORACUM is situated at the confluence of the rivers Ouse and Foss near the centre of Great Britain, and in one of the most rich and extensive valleys in England. It is the capital of the great county to which it gives its name, the see of an archbishop, who is primate and metropolitan of England, and the second city in rank in the kingdom.

E.BAINE
Baine's Yorkshire, vol.2
1969

BLACK SWAN PUB
PEASHOLME GREEN

The coaching station is constructed in a prisoners' workroom, and houses the 1820 stage coach that last ran from Stockton to York with four passengers cramped inside and ten in no great comfort outside.

A timetable announces the York to London coach setting forth from the Black Swan in Coney Street at five in the morning 'and the whole journey takes five days, if God permits'.

R. PATTERSON Quoted in A. STACPOOLE, *The Noble City of York* 1972

York Railway Station

Acknowledgements

Every effort has been made to secure permissions from copyright owners to use the extracts of text featured in this book.

Any subsequent correspondence should be sent to Jarrold Publishing at the following address:
Jarrold Publishing, Whitefriars, Norwich NR3 1TR.

page

12 (left) From *Baine's Yorkshire*, vol 2 by E. Baine. David and Charles Ltd, 1823, reprint 1969.

18 (right) From *The Noble City of York* by A. Stacpoole, 1972.

20 (right) As page 18 (right).

29 As page 12 (left).

27 As page 18 (right)

30 (left) From *Yorkshire: York and the East Riding* by Nikolaus Pevsner, Penguin, 1972, reprinted 1985, copyright © Nikolaus Pevsner, 1972.

35 (left) From *York: The History and Heritage of a City* by R.K. Booth. Barrie & Jenkins, 1990. Used by permission of The Random House Group Ltd.

35 (right) As page 12 (left).

36 (right) As page 18 (right).

39 (left) From *In Praise of Yorkshire* by E. Slingsby, 1951.

39 (right) As page 12 (left).

40 (left) As page 18 (right).

40 (right) As page 12 (left).

43 As page 18 (right).

44 As page 12 (left).

47 (left) As page 12 (left).

52 (right) As page 30 (left).

55 As page 18 (right).

58 As page 35 (left).

61 As page 12 (left).

63 (left) As page 18 (right).

63 (right) As page 12 (left).

64 (left) As page 18 (right).

64 (right) As page 12 (left).

66 *From *The King's England: Yorkshire East Riding and York City* by Arthur Mee. Caxton, 1947. Reproduced by tkind permission of The King's England Press.

70 (left) As page 35 (left).

70 (right) As page 12 (left).

73 (left) As page 35 (left).

73 (right) As page 12 (left).

74 (left) As page 66.

74 (right) As page 39 (left).

76 As page 18 (right).

78 (left) As page 35 (left).

78 (right) As page 39 (left).

80 As page 12 (left).

83 (left) As page 66.

83 (right) As page 39 (left).

84 (top) As page 66.

84 (bottom) As page 39 (left).

87 As page 66.

88 As page 30 (left).

91 (left) As page 12 (left).

93 (left) As page 18 (right).

93 (right) As page 35 (left).

94 (right) As page 66.

97 As page 35 (left).

98 (right) As page 12 (left).

100 As page 18 (right).

102 As page 18 (right).

105 (left) As page 18 (right).

105 (right) As page 12 (left).

106 As page 18 (right).

109 (left) As page 12 (left).

110 As page 18 (right).

113 (left) As page 35 (left).

113 (right) As page 12 (left).

114 As page 30 (left).

116 As page 66.

118 (left) As page 18 (right).

118 (right) As page 12 (left).

* The King's England Press is currently reprinting all of Arthur Mee's King's England county guidebooks in a facsimile of the original 1936–1953 editions.

Bibliography

Stained Glass Window, All Saints North Street

Baine, E.: *Baine's Yorkshire: vol. 2, East and North Ridings*, David and Charles Ltd/S. R. Publishers, 1823. Reprinted 1969.

Bede: *The Ecclesiastical History of the English People*, introduction by Vida D. Scudder, London: J.M. Dent; New York E.P. Dutton, 1910.

Booth, R. K.: *York: The History and Heritage of a City*, Barrie & Jenkins, 1990.

Defoe, Daniel: *Robinson Crusoe*, Penguin, 1994. First published in 1720.

Dickens, Charles: *Nicholas Nickleby*, Penguin, 1994. First published in 1838.

Gaskell, Elizabeth: *Sylvia's Lovers*, Penguin, 1996. First published in 1863.

Mee, Arthur (ed.): *Yorkshire: East Riding and York City*. First published by Caxton in 1947.

Pevsner, Nikolaus: *Yorkshire: York & The East Riding*, Penguin, 1985. First published in 1972.

Slingsby, Eleanor (ed.): *In Praise of Yorkshire*, Camelot, 1951.

Stacpoole, Dom. A.: *The Noble City of York*, Cerialis, 1972.

Sterne, Laurence: *Tristram Shandy*, Penguin, 1997. First published in 1759.

Victoria History of the Counties of England: City of York, vol. 4.

Above: The Water Tower
Opposite: Riverside buildings

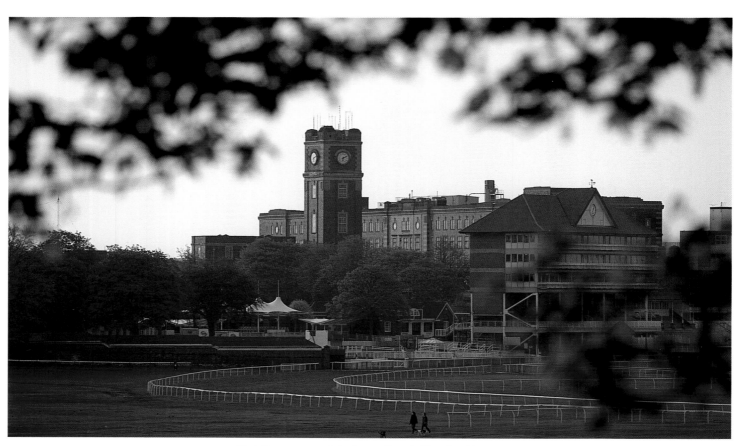

York Racecourse and the former Terry's Chocolate Factory

Index

The Jorvik Centre

GROUNDCOVER
SERIES